The Quotation Bank for A-Level

A Streetcar Named Desire

Tennessee Williams

Copyright © 2023 Esse Publishing Limited and Elaine McNally
The moral rights of the authors have been asserted.

First published in 2022 by:
The Quotation Bank
Esse Publishing Limited
10 9 8 7 6 5 4 3 2

All rights reserved. No part of this publication may be reproduced, resold, stored in a retrieval system or transmitted in any form, or by any means (electronic, photocopying, mechanical or otherwise) without the prior written permission of both the copyright owners and the publisher.

A CIP catalogue record for this book is available from the British Library.
ISBN 978-1-9999816-8-6

All enquiries to: contact@thequotationbank.co.uk
Every effort has been made to trace and contact all relevant copyright holders. However, if contacted the publisher will rectify any omission or error at the earliest opportunity.

Printed and bound by Target Print Limited, Broad Lane, Cottenham, Cambridge CB24 8SW.

www.thequotationbank.co.uk

Introduction

How The Quotation Bank can help you in your exams	4
How to use The Quotation Bank	5

Quotations

Scenes One and Two	6
Scenes Three and Four	12
Scenes Five and Six	16
Scenes Seven and Eight	20
Scenes Nine to Eleven	24
Critical and Contextual Quotations	31

Revision and Essay Planning

Performance History	41
How to revise effectively	42
Suggested revision activities	43
Glossary	44

Welcome to The Quotation Bank, the comprehensive guide to all the key quotations you need to succeed in your exams.

Whilst you may have read the play, watched a film adaptation, understood the plot and have a strong grasp of context, all questions in your A-Levels require you to write a focused essay, full of textual references and quotations (be they textual, critical or contextual), and most importantly, quotations that you then analyse.

I think we all agree it is **analysis** that is the tricky part – and that is why we are here to help!

The Quotation Bank takes 25 of the most important quotations from the text, interprets them, analyses them, highlights literary and dramatic techniques Williams has used, puts them in context, and suggests which quotations you might use in which essays. We have also included 10 contextual and critical quotations, analysed them, and linked them closely to the text, all for you to explore.

At the end of **The Quotation Bank** we have put together a performance history and great revision exercises to help you prepare for your exam. We have also included a detailed glossary to make sure you completely understand what certain literary terms actually mean!

How The Quotation Bank can help you in your exams.

The Quotation Bank is designed to make sure every point you make in an essay clearly fulfils the Assessment Objectives an examiner will be using when marking your work.

Every quotation comes with the following detailed material:

Interpretation: The interpretation of each quotation allows you to fulfil **AO1**, articulating an informed, personal response, and **AO5**, using different interpretations to inform your exploration of the text.

Techniques: Using associated concepts and terminology (in this case, the techniques used by Williams) is a key part of **AO1**, and can help you identify and analyse ways in which meanings are shaped (**AO2**).

Analysis: We have provided as much analysis (**AO2**) as possible, as well as exploring the significance and influence of contextual material (**AO3**) and different interpretations (**AO5**). It is a great idea to analyse the quotation in detail – you need to do more than just say what it means, but also try to explore a variety of different ways of interpreting it.

Use in essays on… Your answer needs to be focused to fulfil **AO1**. This section helps you choose relevant quotations and link them together for a stronger, more detailed essay.

How to use The Quotation Bank.

Many students spend time learning quotations by heart. This can be useful, but it is important to remember what you are meant to do with quotations once you get into the exam.

By using **The Quotation Bank**, not only will you have a huge number of textual, critical and contextual quotations to use in your essays, you will also have ideas on what to say about them, how to analyse them, how to link them together, and what questions to use them for.

These quotations can form the basis of your answer, making sure every point **articulates an informed, personal response (AO1)** and allows you to **analyse ways in which meanings are shaped (AO2)**.

The critical and contextual quotations allow you to easily and effectively explore the significance and influence of **context (AO3)**, and provide you with a variety of **different readings to explore (AO5).**

The textual quotations cover the whole text to allow you to show comprehensive whole text knowledge, and the critical and contextual quotations cover the full range of the text's publication history to help you explore the contexts in which the text was both **written and received (AO3)**.

Epigraph from "The Broken Tower" by Hart Crane:
> "And so it was I entered the broken world
> To trace the visionary company of love, its voice
> An instant in the wind (I know not whither hurled)
> But not for long to hold each desperate choice."

Interpretation: A speaker seeks revelation in a setting that is hostile to love. Crane, a gay man who lived a turbulent life and committed suicide, was a literary hero of Williams.

Techniques: Metaphor; Semantic Field; Personification.

Analysis:
- The metaphor "broken world" is part of a semantic field of fragility that evokes a threatening, discordant place (the play's setting) where love cannot survive.
- Love is personified as a transitory "voice", which lasts only "an instant" then is "hurled", highlighting that the helpless speaker is subject to the caprice of fate.
- Brief affairs that are "not for long" and are a "desperate choice" suggest reality is misery and despair. We recall Blanche's promiscuity and Allan Grey, the poet.

Use in essays on… Desire; Death; Reality and Illusion; Fate and Tragedy.

Scene One:
STANLEY: "Meat!" *He heaves the package at her. She cries out in protest but manages to catch it: then she laughs breathlessly.*

Interpretation: Stanley's first appearance defines his power and potential aggression. He is the antithesis of Blanche, described as a "moth". The audience are confronted with his primitive, brutal sexuality defined later by Blanche as something "sub-human…ape-like".

Techniques: Exclamations; Staging; Innuendo.

Analysis:
- The exclamatory, minor sentence "meat" encapsulates Stanley's confidence. He behaves like a prehistoric hunter with his kill, and his potent masculinity is defined through images of conquest and violence; the package is "red-stained". Stanley is contrasted to other versions of masculinity: Mitch and Allan Grey.
- The direction "heaves the package at her" establishes stereotypical gender roles. Stanley is proprietorial. Stella accepts his dominance and alpha male status.
- Stella delights in the sexual innuendo, as do the Negro Woman and Eunice. This place is crass and vulgar, but there is a frank acceptance of sexuality.

Use in essays on… Desire; Social Class; Violence and Cruelty; Gender; Sexuality.

Scene One:
> **BLANCHE:** "They told me to take a street-car named Desire, and then transfer to one called Cemeteries and ride six blocks and get off at – Elysian Fields!"

Interpretation: There is an inevitability about a journey that starts with desire and ineluctably travels towards Elysian Fields, the land of the Dead in Greek mythology, suggesting the relentless trajectory of classical tragedy.

Techniques: Metaphor; Motif.

Analysis:
- The streetcar brings her to Stanley who is linked to the locomotive. Both forms of transport become metaphors for inescapable modernity and inevitability of fate. The journey is an allegory for Blanche's spiritual decline and tragic fall.
- A psychoanalytic reading reveals conflict between the psychic instincts of Eros and Thanatos that Freud believed drove human behaviour, suggesting other binaries between life and death, creation and destruction, physical and spiritual.
- "Desire" and "Cemeteries" unite sex and death which are recurring motifs in the play, and place it in the context of the Liebestod tradition.

Use in essays on…Desire; Death; Fate and Tragedy.

Scene One:
> **BLANCHE:** "I, I, I took the blows in my face and my body! All of those deaths! The long parade to the graveyard!"

Interpretation: The destruction of Blanche's wealthy, elegant world is traumatic. The splendid mansion, Belle Reve, is now a lost place of ghosts, death and gothic horror.

Techniques: Metaphor; Exclamations; Motif; Sentence Structure.

Analysis:
- This harrowing reproach is conveyed through the metaphor of injury and trauma. Loss is felt as a physical wounding. The antidote to death is desire as Blanche will reveal to Mitch in Scene 9 when confronted with her promiscuity.
- Sentence fragments and exclamations convey her personal decline that parallels the ruin of her home and highlights her precarious mental state and suffering.
- Motifs of death and disease inform the Southern Gothic genre and are recurring motifs in Williams' play. Blanche's tale of illness eroding the splendour of Belle Reve echoes Poe's gothic horror 'The Fall of the House of Usher'.

Use in essays on… Death; Past and Present; Reality and Illusion.

Scene One:

BLANCHE: "Yes, accuse me! Sit there and stare at me, thinking I let the place go! I let the place go? Where were you! In bed with your – Polack!"

Interpretation: Blanche's monologue describes the humiliating loss of Belle Reve, and the miserable life on a ruined plantation which left her with anxieties around death.

Techniques: Exclamations; Questioning; Imperative; Repetition.

Analysis:
- The exclamations, imperatives and combative questions reveal Blanche's resentment and fury. She is bitter about the responsibility that was left to her. The repetition of "I let the place go" reveals her hurt and exasperation.
- There is jealously in the accusation that Stella neglected Blanche and class-based conflict in "Polack". Yet, Stella's life with Stanley offers escape and hope.
- Belle Reve is a metonym for the ruined Southern States. It is a place where "the grim reaper had put up his tent". Blanche is connected to these images of death whereas Stella, "in bed with her Polack", is connected to the future and life.

Use in essays on… Desire; Class; Death; Past and Present.

Scene Two:

Blanche comes out of the bathroom in a red satin robe.

Interpretation: This choice of outfit seems provocative, and she appears unaware of Stanley's rage and suspicion. Considering the play in performance is important: how intentional is Blanche here? In what ways are character and tragedy linked in this scene?

Techniques: Staging; Motif.

Analysis:
- Colour is a recurring motif. "Red" connotes danger, passion, blood and heat, and "satin" extravagance and luxury. Blanche seems seductive and flirtatious. We recall a 'scarlet woman', and The Whore of Babylon in Revelations: 17. The associations are deliberate; Stanley hints at prostitution at the Flamingo. In Scene 6 she ironically uses the invitation of a Parisian call girl to seduce Mitch.
- Her manipulative posturing and play acting, and contradictory character, are evident in costume changes. Blanche wears a "white suit" (suggesting sterility and emptiness), "a flowered print dress", and "a light blue satin kimono" to construct different roles.

Use in essays on…Desire; Reality and Illusion; Fate and Tragedy.

Scene Three:
> *THE POKER NIGHT. There is a picture of Van Gogh's of a billiard-parlour at night. The kitchen now suggests that sort of lurid nocturnal brilliance…*

Interpretation: 'The Night Café' is a painting by Van Gogh that he described as 'the ugliest I've done' and referred to the people in it as 'ruffians'. Williams connects the painting with the staging of a sordid scene with disreputable characters. 'The Poker Night' was one of the original titles for the play, highlighting its centrality.

Techniques: Staging; Metaphor.

Analysis:
- Williams' staging creates a powerful visual impact. "Nocturnal brilliance" is augmented by brash and garish coloured shirts, "watermelon" and "yellow linoleum". "Lurid" connotes an unrefined, tawdry setting with underlying cruelty.
- The poker game is a metaphor for life in this urban setting. Poker involves taking chances, and is dependent on luck or fate. Later Stanley, in Scene 11, will say, "Luck is believing you're lucky". Stanley's belief that he makes his own luck, and controls his own destiny, makes him powerful at this game and in life.

Use in essays on… Violence and Cruelty; Fate and Tragedy; Gender.

Scene Four:
   Outside, a train approaches...Under cover of the train's noise Stanley enters.

Interpretation: The train or locomotive is associated with Stanley in the play. Here, the sound of the train creates dramatic irony as it allows Stanley to enter unseen. It is an aspect of William's 'plastic theatre' which led him to use staging in non-naturalistic ways.

Techniques: Dramatic Irony; Symbolism; Plastic Theatre; Motif.

Analysis:
- The train connotes modernity and power, so is a fitting symbol for Stanley. It is also, through literary associations with, for example, Tolstoy's 'Anna Karenina', a symbol of fate, and Stanley is positioned as Blanche's' nemesis.
- The train is a phallic symbol augmenting Stanley's dominant masculinity. It is the "roar of an approaching locomotive" in Scene 10 that creates a mood of disturbance, threat and menace prior to the brutal rape.
- The train motif reminds us of the "streetcar", the symbol of fate and destructive desire in the play, and which has brought Blanche to Stanley.

Use in essays on... Death; Fate and Tragedy; Guilt.

Scene Four:

BLANCHE: "Such things as art – as poetry and music – such kinds of new light have come into the world…Don't – don't hang back with the brutes!"

Interpretation: Civilization and art (genteel Blanche) conflicts with brutish materialism (atavistic Stanley). Blanche's stylized prose is juxtaposed to the "grunting" of "brutes".

Techniques: Juxtaposition; Imperative.

Analysis:

- Blanche is an English teacher: she is cultured, but she is ill-equipped for the modern world which she sees as regressive. Her interest is in a Romantic search for truth and beauty that underpins her many literary references.
- "Art" is juxtaposed with "brutes". This structural binary is a clash between the Apollonian (progress, order, civilisation) and Dionysian (disorder, intoxication, ecstasy) which Nietzsche saw as the catalyst for tragedy.
- The imperatives convey the fear that motivates Blanche and compels her to warn her sister. Blanche believes that life with Stanley is a terrible compromise.

Use in essays on… Reality and Illusion; Social Class.

Scene Four:

Stella has embraced him with both arms, fiercely, and full in the view of Blanche. He laughs and clasps her head to him. Over her head he grins ... at Blanche.

Interpretation: Stanley is victorious as Stella ignores Blanche's criticism of her feelings as "brutal desire". Stella defiantly chooses love and domestic security over sisterly loyalty.

Techniques: Language; Tableaux Vivant.

Analysis:
- Desire drives Stella too, suggested by the adverb "fiercely". "Full in the view" is insolent; she defiantly stands by her love for Stanley, and seems aroused by his violence. How do you judge the choice Stella makes? How sympathetic is she?
- Stanley's Machiavellian "grin" and laughter stress his cruel triumph. He is determined to defeat Blanche and is ruthless in his pursuit of victory.
- Each scene is like a one act play, ending on a moment of dramatic tension: a tableaux vivant. This moment demonstrates that Stella can shift the balance of power, and is the battleground over which Stanley and Blanche fight.

Use in essays on... Desire; Gender; Guilt.

Scene Five:

> BLANCHE: "And so the soft people have got to - shimmer and glow - put a - paper lantern over the light...But I'm scared now - awf'ly scared. I don't know how much longer I can turn the trick."

Interpretation: This is a harrowing confession, despite the euphemistic language. Women are valued for their youth and beauty, and Blanche recognises she is aging.

Techniques: Metaphor; Irony; Euphemism.

Analysis:

- The paper lantern is a metaphor for the "glow" of youth and desirability. Later, both Mitch and Stanley will cruelly rip the real paper lantern that shields Blanche, who fears aging, from confronting ugly reality and harsh truth.
- Ironically, Blanche exploits the sexuality she feels degrades her to attract the attention she craves. Is she "scared", or is this an aspect of her role playing? Is she deliberately manipulative, deceptive, and behaving with risky promiscuity?
- The colloquial idiom "turn the trick" hints ominously at prostitution, not just the conjuring of magic or illusion. Blanche, too, is guilty of "epic fornications".

Use in essays on... Reality and Illusion; Gender; Fate and Tragedy; Desire.

Scene Five:
> **BLANCHE:** "Honey lamb. Come here! ... I want to kiss you – just once – softly and sweetly on your mouth…I've got to be good and keep my hands off children."

Interpretation: Despite claiming to want "to rest", which Mitch offers her, Blanche continuously rejects material and emotional security, and recklessly pursues sexual desire.

Techniques: Imagery; Innuendo; Imperative.

Analysis:

- The flirtation with the "young man" is unsettling. The gustatory imagery "honey lamb", along with the innuendo "you make my mouth water", is erotic, sensual and deliberately seductive. Is it possible to retain sympathy for Blanche here?
- Blanche is predatory; the imperatives suggest intense desire. Her character is contradictory. The prim behaviour she adopts with Mitch conceals the addictive and self-destructive sexual passion that inexorably leads her to tragedy.
- The disclosure about her past shows just how wayward she has been, and foreshadows Stanley's revelations about what has happened in Laurel.

Use in essays on…Desire; Reality and Illusion; Fate and Tragedy.

Scene Six:

Blanche speaks with an affectation of demureness. "You may release me now... I said unhand me, sir."

Interpretation: Blanche metatheatrically performs the role of a virtuous and bashful Southern Belle, investing Mitch with the illusion of gallantry and chivalry. Blanche needs make-believe to bear the ugliness and ordinariness of her blighted life.

Techniques: Tone; Irony.

Analysis:

- The role is another disguise, it is "an affectation", and there is an exaggerated artifice about her coquettish tone. The film *'Gone with the Wind'* crystalised the aristocratic elegance of the antebellum South with its ideals of femininity.
- This role is anachronistic and ironically places Blanche in a destroyed past. The South was defeated in the Civil War. Its plantation culture was built on the horror of enslavement; under the sophisticated façade was a rotten society. Similarly, Blanche dishonestly and knowingly plays this role to beguile Mitch.

Use in essays on... Reality and Illusion; Past and Present; Social Class; Gender.

Scene Six:
MITCH: "You need somebody. And I need somebody, too. Could it be – you and me, Blanche?"

Interpretation: Mitch's proposal gives Blanche the safe haven she desires. Mitch can be awkward and clownish, but here his gentle sympathy and kindness is revealed.

Techniques: Modal verb; Irony.

Analysis:
- Mitch is fascinated by Blanche; yet, he is dull and ordinary, and her intellectual inferior. His tentative language, the modal verb "could", and the pause reveal his uncertainty and nervousness.
- The parallelism "you need / I need" shows their similarities. They have both loved and lost, and seek comfort. Yet, despite her gratitude and acceptance, it seems unlikely that Blanche would settle for monogamous marriage with Mitch.
- Ironically, Blanche gets this proposal by telling the truth, not through deception, but we hear the locomotive and polka music suggesting her fate is preordained.

Use in essays on…Social Class; Fate and Tragedy.

Scene Seven:
BLANCHE: "Possess your soul in patience!" STANLEY: "It's not my soul I'm worried about!"

Interpretation: Blanche's occupation of the bathroom is driving Stanley crazy. This exchange is comical. The juxtaposition of comic and tragic moods heightens the tension.

Techniques: Dramatic Irony; Repetition; Exclamations.

Analysis:
- The crude, sarcastic humour (there are comedic moments in this play), reveals Stanley wants the toilet. The repetition of "soul" draws attention to Blanche and Stanley as opposites. The soul and its association with beauty, truth, and spirituality is set against the physical; the body and its raw, obscene processes.
- The line hints at Blanche's immorality which Stanley has revealed to Stella. Blanche is oblivious to Stanley's hostility, but we are alert to the dramatic irony.
- Both lines end in exclamation marks but generate different moods. How might an actor shape our interpretation from the way these lines are delivered?

Use in essays on… Desire; Reality and Illusion; Gender.

Scene Seven:
BLANCHE: "Oh, I feel so good after my long, hot bath, I feel so good and cool and – rested!"

Interpretation: Blanche's compulsive bathing symbolises a desire to be cleansed. Williams has structured this episode 'contrapuntally'. Stanley's shocking revelations occur together with Blanche's singing in the bath. Does this make us pity Blanche?

Techniques: Staging; Tri-colon (or list of three); Assonance; Repetition; Irony.

Analysis:
- The staging of the cramped flat and tiny, shared bathroom emphasises the restricted space in which Stanley and Blanche struggle for territory.
- The list of three, assonance and elongated vowels create a languid, affected tone. Blanche seems content, but the stage directions indicate "a frightened look" on her face, suggesting her leisurely elegance is an orchestrated pose.
- Blanche is haunted by guilt. The repetition of "good" is ironic; despite the ritual cleansing Blanche is unable to purify herself. The spilled coke also suggests this.

Use in essays on…Reality and Illusion; Guilt; Past and Present.

Scene Eight:
   STANLEY: "I am not a Polack...what I am is a one hundred percent American, born and raised in the greatest country on earth."

Interpretation: Stanley's fury escalates as he defends himself against Blanche's snobbery and prejudice. Is Stanley presented sympathetically as he opposes Blanche's xenophobia?

Techniques: Language; Metaphor.

Analysis:
- Stanley's working-class pride, machismo and fervent patriotism is evident in his assertive declaratives. The superlative "greatest" conveys his admiration for the country he fought for in WWII and which offers him the chance to prosper.
- Stanley's ambition is fiscal security and material success, emphasised by the numerical metaphor he uses boastfully to describe himself.
- Engraved on the Statue of Liberty are lines from Emma Lazarus's 'The New Colossus' that evoke the world Stanley believes in. As an immigrant's son, he embodies the American dream and its egalitarian opportunities for success.

Use in essays on... Social Class; Past and Present; Gender.

Scene Eight:
STANLEY: "I pulled you down off them columns and how you loved it, having them coloured lights going!"

Interpretation: Class conscious Stanley reminds Stella of her upbringing at Belle Reve, and brags about humbling her. The Doric columns are from a plantation mansion.

Techniques: Metaphor; Juxtaposition.

Analysis:
- Stanley is a powerful force for change. "I pulled you" underscores his thriving vitality juxtaposed to the static, moribund South represented by the "columns".
- The clash between old and new explored through sexual tension and class can be seen in Strindberg's *'Miss Julie'* which has many similarities with Streetcar. Jean the footman says to Miss Julie (who imagines being on top of a pillar) "Fall to my level and then I can pick you up again".
- A proposed title was 'The Primary Colors' and the metaphor of "colored lights" conveys the intense passion between Stella and Stanley. Theirs is a world of brash colour and life, unlike Blanche's which is the effete sterility of whiteness.

Use in essays on... Desire; Death; Social Class; Sexuality.

Scene Nine:
> *The rapid, feverish polka tune, the 'Varsouviana' is heard. The music is in her mind; she is drinking to escape it and the sense of disaster closing in on her.*

Interpretation: As an aspect of William's plastic theatre, the polka tune conjures an inner psychological state in a non-naturalistic way. It symbolises Blanche's guilt about the suicide of Allan Grey, but is also heard at moments of desperation or crisis.

Techniques: Plastic Theatre; Adjective; Symbolism.

Analysis:
- Williams saw his plays as 'memory plays'. The polka tune is an expressionist technique that moves Blanche between past memories and the present. It amplifies the inevitability of Blanche's fate as she cannot escape past trauma.
- Mitch will soon cruelly reject her. The tune has become "rapid, feverish", adjectives that augment the impeding catastrophe and her agitated emotions.
- The Varsouviana is also linked to her fragile mental state and at the end, in her madness, its sound becomes nightmarish and jarring as she deteriorates.

Use in essays on… Madness; Fate and Tragedy; Guilt; Past and Present.

Scene Nine:
BLANCHE: "I don't tell truth, I tell what ought to be truth. And if that is sinful, then let me be damned for it."

Interpretation: Blanche concedes she lies, although her language is typically evasive and oblique as she defends her "magic" to Mitch over the "realism" that is so painful for her.

Techniques: Tone; Symbolism; Imagery; Repetition.

Analysis:
- The word "truth" is used ambiguously, and repetition distorts its meaning. "If" allows her to prevaricate and, despite the explicitly Christian imagery, avoid moral judgements, perpetuating escapist fantasies and justifying her behaviour.
- Blanche is an aesthete; she seeks beauty and places that above conventional morality. Like Oscar Wilde, who said 'Lying, the telling of beautiful untrue things, is the proper aim of art', Blanche disingenuously defends her manipulation of the truth. Truth is symbolised by the light of the naked bulb that Blanche screens with the lantern, and which Mitch will violently tear off.

Use in essays on… Reality and Illusion; Violence and Cruelty; Guilt.

Scene Ten:
STANLEY: "Tiger – tiger! Drop the bottle-top! Drop it! We've had this date with each other from the beginning!"

Interpretation: Stanley appears to see events as part of a rough mating ritual and is unconcerned about attacking his wife's sister.

Techniques: Imperative; Pronouns; Symbolism.

Analysis:
- Calling her "tiger" fetishes her terror and sexualizes her desperate defense with the broken bottle. The imperatives convey dominance, the plural pronoun implies mutuality, and "date" is ambiguous, suggesting both a predetermined event and romantic encounter, allowing Stanley to justify and blur his brutality.
- This scene is complicated by the film, in which a charismatic Marlon Brando generated sympathy for Stanley. The rape scene was edited to be less explicit.
- The rape can symbolise the total annihilation of the Southern way of life by the modern, industrial North. Blanche threatens his territory and must be destroyed.

Use in essays on…Desire; Violence and Cruelty; Past and Present.

Scene Eleven:
STELLA: "I couldn't believe her story and go on living with Stanley". **EUNICE:** "…Life has got to go on. No matter what happens you've got to keep on going."

Interpretation: Stella is resolved to hold on to Stanley. The alternative is the crumbling world of Belle Reve. Her choice to reject her sister seems motivated by self-preservation.

Techniques: Repetition; Motif; Juxtaposition; Structure.

Analysis:
- Repetition of "go" and "going" takes us back to the streetcar and its inevitable journey. Motifs of relentless forward motion structure the play. Eunice and Stella subscribe to this brutal Darwinian universe where the survivors are those who look forward, accommodating themselves to change and modernity.
- Stella too prefers illusion rather than reality at the end. Her words juxtapose the conflict between Blanche and Stanley, making her sister the enemy. Marriage and motherhood give her purpose, whereas Blanche offers only the decadence and decay of a rotten inheritance. Are Stella's choices selfish? Is she submissive?

Use in essays on… Gender; Past and Present; Guilt.

Scene Eleven:

BLANCHE: "I'm going to die on the sea…[*The cathedral chimes are heard.*] And I'll be buried at sea sewn up in a clean white sack and dropped overboard…"

Interpretation: Blanche, who has slipped into madness, fantasises about her death in a peaceful and lyrical speech replete with religious symbolism.

Techniques: Motif; Symbolism; Repetition; Sibilance.

Analysis:

- Linking death and water connotes purification, augmented by water's association with rebirth and baptism. The "clean white sack" reveals a longing for absolution. Water is a recurring motif, and Blanche's many baths symbolise a desire to wash away guilt perhaps linked to the suicide of Allan Grey.
- The repetition of "sea" and "die", the sibilance of "sea", "sewn", "sack", and the mournful, yet untroubling chime of bells present death as a gentle release.
- Blanche can be seen in the tradition of Shakespearean tragic heroines. Stanley sarcastically calls her "Queen of the Nile" or Cleopatra. Finally, she reminds us of Ophelia, driven to madness and a watery grave.

Use in essays on…Madness; Reality and Illusion; Fate and Tragedy; Death.

Scene Eleven:
   STANLEY: [*voluptuously, soothingly*]: "Now, honey. Now, love. Now, now love."

Interpretation: This final tableau disturbingly combines guilt and distress with arousal and pleasure. Stella seems to submit to Stanley's dominant masculinity, disappointing us in her silent passivity and possible acceptance. Stanley is re-established as alpha male.

Techniques: Staging; Language; Repetition.

Analysis:
- The stage direction "voluptuously" suggests sexual pleasure, reminding us of Stella sobbing "luxuriously", adverbs that connote sensuality and indulgence.
- The repetition of "Love" blurs its connotations and use; is it a noun or an imperative? Is it used patronisingly or romantically? It seems that it is not love as a spiritual, sacred emotion that triumphs, but "brutal desire".
- The repetition of "now" draws attention to the present. It is modernity embodied in the vitality of an immigrant that is the final image, augmenting the possibility of changing social structures in a new world.

Use in essays on… Desire; Social Class; Past and Present; Gender; Sexuality.

Scene Eleven:

> **STEVE: "This game is seven-card stud."**

Interpretation: The last line of the play is given to Steve, who plays poker, jokes crudely and rows with Eunice. In his drunkenness, violence and lechery, Steve is what might become of Stanley in the future, all of which suggests a bleak ending to the play.

Techniques: Metaphor; Imagery; Motif.

Analysis:
- Scene 3 established the metaphor of life as a card game. There are recurring motifs of gaming, chance and luck that illuminate the theme of fate. It is the men who play cards and win; this is a patriarchal world where women spectate. Steve's words indicate that life will go on as usual; Blanche will be forgotten.
- The last word is "stud". It refers to poker, but it is also an image of aggressive masculinity. We recall Stanley "the gaudy seed-bearer" and Steve's jokes about hens and roosters. Stanley's virility is confirmed by the child in a "blue blanket" suggesting it is a boy. Blanche has been sacrificed to secure Stanley's future.

Use in essays on… Reality and Illusion; Gender; Fate and Tragedy; Desire.

Tennessee Williams (1939) said,
"I have only one major theme for my work, which is the destructive power of society on the sensitive, non-conformist individual."

Interpretation: This statement uses familiar binaries that structure the play: brute strength/sensitivity, society/individual, binaries that Michael Billington describes as "macho materialism" versus "spiritual and artistic values". Williams uses the tragic mode to show that Blanche's poetry is no match for the crude muscle that inevitably triumphs.

Analysis:
- Madness is one result of a destructive society. Blanche, sensitive and fragile, disintegrates into insanity wearing a "worn out Mardi-Gras outfit" with a "crazy crown", punished because she does not conform to conventional morality.
- Men who offer alternative versions of masculinity are sensitive. Mitch is gentle, treasuring the case with its poetic dedication. Allan Grey is a poet, and a gay man, who committed suicide. Society will not allow these men success.
- Tischler said Williams was "a poet in a practical world": a nonconformist, artistic, sensitive, an obsessive hypochondriac and worried about hereditary mental illness because of his sister's insanity.

Use in essays on… Reality and Illusion; Madness; Gender; Violence and Cruelty.

In a letter to Eric Bentley, Williams (1948) wrote,
"the use of transparencies and music and subtle lighting effects…were dismissed as 'cheap tricks and devices.' All of these plastic things are as valid instruments of expression in the theatre as words."

Interpretation: Williams combines techniques from naturalistic and expressionist theatre to move beyond realism, to create "a more penetrating and vivid expression of things as they are". This is Williams's plastic theatre which expresses subliminal states, and disrupts the exterior verisimilitude, giving us access to interior lives of characters.

Analysis:

- Williams insists his theatre should exploit all its aspects to create aural and visual effects so that intangible experiences are visible to the audience. He notes these are as important as "words", suggesting their power to make meaning.
- The blue piano, polka tune, the train, "lurid reflections" and "inhuman voices" create a theatrical experience that gives insight into the human condition.
- The plastic theatre elements make evident the fragmentation of Blanche's mind. They amplify the tragic emotions of pity and fear for the audience.

Use in essays on… Reality and Illusion.

> **Logan Gourlay, reviewing the play in 1949, criticised the play as,**
> **"the progress of a prostitute, the flight of a nymphomaniac, the ravings of a sexual neurotic."**

Interpretation: Responses to Blanche have evolved. Gourlay is appalled at the sensationalist and repugnant sexual content – Blanche is sleazy and perverse, her behaviour salacious and transgressive. Modern productions see more complexity in Blanche. Susannah Clapp described Gillian Anderson in the role as "utterly compelling".

Analysis:
- Vivian Leigh, who also played Scarlett O'Hara, the archetypal Southern Belle, was synonymous with Blanche, investing her with subdued dignity in the final scene. The iconic "I have always depended on the kindness of strangers" shows Blanche's final retreat into a fantasy South with chivalric gentleman callers.
- Gillian Anderson said, "I thought Leigh's Blanche was…weak, in a way. My Blanche…comes with a lot of gusto and oomph". What was condemned as "ravings" has become strength. We are sensitive to Blanche's disintegration as a response to persecution and trauma, and challenge stereotypes about gender.

Use in essays on…Desire; Gender; Madness.

Arthur Miller (1958) argues,
"The structure of a play is always the story of how the birds came home to roost."

Interpretation: Miller, a contemporary of Williams, argues a play is structured around the past events that bring a character into the present looking for safety: a home in which to "roost". Conflict is caused by past actions or events intruding into the present.

Analysis:
- The word "always" connotes inevitability, thereby suggesting that the return of the past is destined. Miller's argument echoes Donald Pease who stated that, "for Williams the act of fleeing always becomes the act of relieving the past".
- The structure of the play, with its 11 scenes, moves relentlessly forward, but also uses episodic flashbacks, showing us the catastrophes and sorrow that have brought Blanche to this point. Her return and eventual doom are preordained.
- Blanche is looking for "rest" and a place to "breathe quietly" but the "home" she comes to is not hers but Stanley's. Ironically, Blanche will not find the paradisiacal home she seeks in "Elysian Fields", except perhaps only the final home of an asylum, then oblivion and death.

Use in essays on… Death; Past and Present; Fate and Tragedy.

Gore Vidal (1985) wrote,
"In 1947, when Marlon Brando appeared on stage in a torn sweaty T-shirt, there was an earthquake."

Interpretation: Marlon Brando's electrifying portrayal of Stanley, both on stage and in the 1951 film, mythologised the sexual potency of the working-class hero whose virility would revitalize a decadent culture. Despite being the villain, Brando made the character sympathetic, with emotional complexity. Early theatre audiences cheered at the rape.

Analysis:
- Brando's huge magnetism is suggested by the hyperbole of the metaphor "earthquake", underscoring his erotic attraction and sexual potency. In the film, his swaggering entrance wearing a tight T-shirt highlighted his muscularity (and homoerotic appeal), meaning that Brando became synonymous with Stanley.
- The ferocity and beauty of Brando's Stanley is undiminished. In 2020 Woody Allen wrote, "Marlon Brando was a living poem", praising his trailblazing talent.
- Brando's iconic sexual attractiveness and performance complicates the play because Stanley's brutality is conflated with irresistible sexual desire.

Use in essays on… Gender; Class; Desire; Violence and Cruelty.

Nina Leibman (1987) asserts that,
"Stella's sexuality is approved because she is sexual in response to her husband. She is not the lustful instigator but the passive respondent."

Interpretation: Stella represents a traditional model of femininity, adhering to acceptable codes of female behaviour in a misogynistic world. Her submission, and lack of autonomy, implies she is trapped in marriage and a victim of patriarchal oppression.

Analysis:

- Leibman's feminist argument makes Stella more "passive" than the text suggests. Stanley uses the plural pronoun to talk about desire in, "wasn't we happy together", implying mutuality. Is Stella weak and passive? Or is her devotion and desire to preserve her marriage admirable? How does the play present female sexuality?
- Blanche is punished for her transgressive sexuality. She mocks the perception of her as predatory when she refers to "the Tarantula arms" and her "victims". Lust has ruined her whereas Stella's legitimate desire for Stanley is rewarded with life.
- The 1951 film censored scenes that included Stella's delight in Stanley's "animal force" and Blanche's promiscuity, implying female sexuality was problematic.

Use in essays on... Gender; Desire.

Felicia Hardison Londré (1997) argues that when Blanche hands papers to Stanley it is,

> "the evolution of the social system from the old agrarian South…as represented by Blanche, to the post-war urban-industrial society in which Stanley's class has gained leverage."

Interpretation: Hardison Londré's Marxist reading presents the transfer of power as the conflict between a doomed aristocratic class and the burgeoning power of the working class. This has a Darwinian aspect: do we admire Stanley? Does he now have "leverage"?

Analysis:
- The papers are a synecdoche for the "old agrarian South", a decadent, but mythically bucolic civilization founded on enslavement, transferred to the "hands" (another synecdoche for the energetic determination and materialism embodied in the immigrant) of Stanley whose world is industry and commerce.
- When Blanche says, with irony, that, "it's wonderfully fitting that Belle Reve should finally be this bunch of old papers in your big, capable hands" she wryly accepts the loss of power and the deterioration of her way of life.

Use in essays on…Social Class; Past and Present; Death.

Albert Wertheim (2004) observes,
"Williams casts something of a cold eye on the triumph of a new (postwar) South peopled by brutish and insensitive Stanley Kowalskis and their progeny."

Interpretation: Wertheim sees the baby as the symbol of a possibly bleak future, and implies that Williams is not hopeful for a world that celebrates Stanley's victory over Blanche, which is the victory of the North over the South. This victory comes at a cost and through terrible violence. Does Williams criticise a world in which Stanley triumphs?

Analysis:

- Stanley is "brutish and insensitive", but he does love Stella and fights to secure her loyalty. It is significant that the rape of Blanche occurs when Stella's baby is born as it suggests Stanley has triumphed in the microcosm and in the macrocosm.
- The point that Williams "casts a cold eye" is disputable. Stanley lives in New Orleans; this is a multicultural, more egalitarian world which replaces the corrupt, racist culture of the South. His baby is not a DuBois baby and is born into a world of opportunity where power structures are changing.

Use in essays on... Social Class; Past and Present; Violence and Cruelty.

Sean McEvoy (2009) suggests that,
> "the tragedy in this play...lies not in personal circumstances, but in the lives and losses of the culture and the society itself."

Interpretation: McEvoy argues Blanche is not the tragic hero, despite the interplay of character and fate in her downfall. Instead he writes that tragedy lies in the community.

Analysis:
- Elysian Fields is a 'cosmopolitan' place: vibrant, diverse, where determined working class men returning from WWII believed they could build a new life based on American values of liberty and perseverance. Yet, under this ideal America lies a seedy place with drunks, prostitutes, and thieves. McEvoy suggests that the real tragedy is that the American Dream is unachievable, and in the face of struggle and failure "just to carry on is the most tragic thing of all".
- Williams himself might dispute this. He said he wrote of "little people" who live and feel with "intensity" and who therefore have tragic possibility. Arthur Miller wrote, "the common man is as apt a subject for tragedy as kings were". Tragedy does also seem to lie in the personal lives and circumstances of 'little people'.

Use in essays on... Reality and Illusion; Social Class; Fate and Tragedy.

Patricia Hern (2014) argues that,
> "Blanche may be a 'cover' for a male character, a homosexual, given a female mask by Williams."

Interpretation: Hern notes the importance of Williams' homosexuality to his plays. Williams wrote at a time when homosexuality was illegal which may explain his uneasy and defensive attitude towards his sexuality. Hern prompts us to examine why it might be Williams' objective to view Stanley, the male, through female eyes.

Analysis:

- "Cover" and "mask" reminds us of Blanche who wears masks to feign different roles. Stanley claims it is "the same old lines, same old act, same old hooey".
- Williams said, "I must find characters who correspond to my own tensions", and Blanche, potentially a proxy for Williams, incessantly conjures a protective carapace of illusions to withdraw from a world in which she has no place.
- The presentation of homosexuality is worth interrogating. Blanche feels revulsion at finding her husband in bed with another man, Stella describes Allan Grey as "degenerate", and his homosexuality is linked to his death.

Use in essays on… Reality and Illusion; Guilt, Desire and Death.

Performance History

In Elia Kazan's 1947 Broadway production, Jessica Tandy played Blanche as mentally fragile from the play's outset; Stanley simply ensures her inevitable downfall. Reception to Brando's portrayal of Stanley was, by today's standards, troubling; Vidal stated, "when Marlon Brando appeared on stage in a torn sweaty T-shirt, there was an earthquake." Brando's Stanley is physically attractive, alluring, the epitome of 1940s masculinity. When the play hit London, Logan Gourlay's anger was directed not at Stanley but at "the progress of a prostitute, the flight of a nymphomaniac, the ravings of a sexual neurotic."

On tour, Uta Hagen took the role of Blanche, instilling her with mental strength at the outset of the play; Hagen stressed Stanley's role in Blanche's madness, and as the root cause of her mental decline. Gillian Anderson's depiction in 2014 continued this; she argued "My Blanche…comes with a lot of gusto and oomph." This is pertinent when considering Blanche's final line, "I have always depended on the kindness of strangers." Does she arrive already broken by her previous life, entirely reliant on the "kindness of strangers", or is there a final flicker of strength that is cruelly extinguished by Stanley?

Hollywood audiences and censors required a different ending in the 1951 film. Rather than engage with the brutal yet realistic ending, the "sensitive" individual left behind, in this case Stella, emerges defiant whilst Stanley is defeated. Rather than the heavily loaded word "stud", the film ends with Stella stating she is "never going back". Whilst satisfying an audience seeking entertainment, not moral conundrums, Williams disapproved; society was unwilling to face its "destructive power". The film and 1949 Aldwych Theatre production also had to remove reference to Allan Grey's homosexuality. Ironically, Williams illuminates the "destructive power of society on the sensitive, non-conformist individual" and then censors play their part perfectly, eradicating arguably the most vulnerable of all the characters.

How to revise effectively.

One mistake people often make is to try to revise EVERYTHING!

This is clearly not possible.

Instead, once you understand the text in detail, a good idea is to pick five or six major themes, and four or five major characters, and revise these in great detail. The same is true when exploring key scenes – you are unlikely to be able to closely analyse every single line, so focus on the *skills* of analysis and interpretation and then be ready for any question, rather than covering the whole text and trying to pre-prepare everything.

If, for example, you revised Blanche and Past and Present, you will also have covered a huge amount of material to use in questions about Guilt, Reality and Illusion or Death.

It is also sensible to avoid revising quotations in isolation; instead, bring together two or three textual quotations as well as a critical and contextual quotation so that any argument you make is supported and explored in detail.

Finally, make sure material is pertinent to the questions you will be set. By revising the skills of interpretation and analysis you will be able to answer the actual question set in the exam, rather than the one you wanted to come up.

Suggested Revision Activities

A great cover and repeat exercise – Cover the whole page, apart from the quotation at the top. Can you now fill in the four sections without looking – Interpretations, Techniques, Analysis, Use in essays on…?

This also works really well as **a revision activity with a friend** – cover the whole page, apart from the quotation at the top. If you read out the quotation, can they tell you the four sections without looking – Interpretations, Techniques, Analysis, Use in essays on…?

For both activities, could you extend the analysis and interpretation further, or provide an alternative interpretation? Also, can you find another quotation that extends or counters the point you have just made?

Your very own Quotation Bank! Using the same headings and format as The Quotation Bank, find 10 more quotations from throughout the text (select them from many different sections of the text to help develop whole text knowledge) and create your own revision cards.

Essay writing – They aren't always fun, but writing essays is great revision. Devise a practice question and try taking three quotations and writing out a perfect paragraph, making sure you add connectives, technical vocabulary and sophisticated language.

Glossary

Dramatic Irony – When the audience knows something the characters don't: the sound of the train creates dramatic irony as it allows Stanley to enter unseen.

Imagery – Figurative language that appeals to the senses of the audience: the gustatory imagery "honey lamb" is erotic, sensual and deliberately seductive.

Imperative – A sentence that gives a command or an order: the imperatives convey the fear that motivates Blanche, and compels her to warn her sister.

Irony – A statement that suggests one thing but often has a contrary meaning: when Blanche says, with irony, that, "it's wonderfully fitting that Belle Reve should finally be this bunch of old papers in your big, capable hands" she wryly accepts the loss of power and the deterioration of her way of life.

Juxtaposition – Two ideas, images or words placed next to each other to create a contrasting effect: juxtaposition of comic and tragic moods heightens the tension.

Language – The vocabulary chosen to create effect.

Metaphor – A word or phrase used to describe something else so that the first idea takes on the associations of the second: Blanche's harrowing reproach is conveyed through the metaphor of injury and trauma.

Motif – A significant idea, element or symbol repeated throughout the text: "Desire" and "Cemeteries" unite sex and death which are recurring motifs in the play, and place it in the context of the Liebestod tradition.

Personification – A non-human object or concept takes on human qualities to make its presence more vivid to the audience: love is personified as a transitory "voice", which lasts only "An instant" then is "hurled", highlighting that the helpless speaker is subject to the caprice of fate.

Repetition – When a word, phrase or idea is repeated to reinforce it: repetition of "I let the place go" reveals her hurt and exasperation.

Semantic Field – A group of words used together from the same topic area: "broken world" is part of a semantic field of fragility that evokes a threatening, discordant place (the play's setting) where love cannot survive.

Sentence Structure – The way the writer has ordered the words in a sentence to create a certain effect: sentence fragments and exclamations convey her personal decline that parallels the ruin of her home, and highlights her precarious mental state and suffering.

Sibilance – A variation on alliteration, usually of the 's' sound, that creates a hissing sound: the sibilance of "sea", "sewn", "sack", and the mournful, yet untroubling chime of bells present death as a gentle release.

Staging – Directions given to the director or actor to aid interpretation: staging of the cramped flat and tiny, shared bathroom emphasises the restricted space in which Stanley and Blanche struggle for territory.

Symbolism – The use of a symbol to represent an idea: Blanche, who has slipped into madness, fantasises about her death in a peaceful and lyrical speech replete with religious symbolism.

Tri-colon – A list of three words or phrases for effect: "good and cool and – rested" create a languid, affected tone.

Acknowledgements:

T Williams: *The Selected Letters of Tennessee Williams: 1920-1945* and *The Selected Letters of Tennessee Williams: 1946-57*, edited by A J Devlin and N M Tischler, published by New Directions 2002/2004.

L Gourlay: Theatre review from *Sunday Express*, 1949.

A Miller: *Tragedy and the Common Man*, published by The New York Times, 1949.

A Miller: *The Shadows of the Gods: A Critical View of the American Theatre*, published by Harper Magazine, 1958.

G Vidal: *Tennesse Williams: Someone to Laugh at Squares With* from *The New York Review of Books*, 1985.

N Leibman: *Sexual Misdemeanor/Psychoanalytic Felony* from *Cinema Journal: Vol. 26, No. 2*, published by University of Texas Press, 1987.

F Hardison Londré: *A Streetcar Running Fifty Years*, from *The Cambridge Companion to Tennessee Williams*, edited by M Roudane, published by Cambridge University Press, 1997.

A Wertheim: *Staging the War: American Drama and World War II*, published by Indiana University Press, 2004.

N M Tischler: *Romantic Textures in Tennessee Williams' Plays and Short Stories*, from *Bloom's Modern Critical Views: Tennessee Williams*, published by Infobase Publishing, 2007.

M Billington: *Tennessee Williams: The Quiet Revolutionary*, published by *The Guardian*, 2009.

S McEvoy: *Tragedy - A Student Handbook*, published by The English and Media Centre, 2009.

P Hern: *A Student Handbook to the Plays of Tennessee Williams: The Glass Menagerie; A Streetcar Named Desire; Cat on a Hot Tin Roof; Sweet Bird of Youth*, published by Bloomsbury Publishing, 2014.

G Anderson: from an interview with A Akbar, published in *The Guardian*, 2020.